POSTMODERN ENCOUNTERS

Barthes and the Empire of Signs

Peter Pericles Trifonas

Series editor: Richard Appignanesi

ICON BOOKS UK

TOTEM BOOKS USA

Published in the UK in 2001
by Icon Books Ltd., Grange Road,
Duxford, Cambridge CB2 4QF
E-mail: info@iconbooks.co.uk
www.iconbooks.co.uk

Published in the USA in 2001
by Totem Books
Inquiries to: Icon Books Ltd.,
Grange Road, Duxford,
Cambridge CB2 4QF, UK

Sold in the UK, Europe, South Africa
and Asia by Faber and Faber Ltd.,
3 Queen Square, London WC1N 3AU
or their agents

Distributed to the trade in the USA by
National Book Network Inc.,
4720 Boston Way, Lanham,
Maryland 20706

Distributed in the UK, Europe,
South Africa and Asia by
Macmillan Distribution Ltd.,
Houndmills, Basingstoke RG21 6XS

Distributed in Canada by
Penguin Books Canada,
10 Alcorn Avenue, Suite 300,
Toronto, Ontario M4V 3B2

Published in Australia in 2001
by Allen & Unwin Pty. Ltd.,
83 Alexander Street,
Crows Nest, NSW 2065

Series editor: Richard Appignanesi

ISBN 1 84046 277 9

Typesetting by Wayzgoose

Printed and bound in the UK by
Cox & Wyman Ltd., Reading

Semiology, Myth, Culture

Empire of Signs? Yes, if it is understood that these signs are empty and that the ritual is without a god.[1] Roland Barthes

Empire of Signs, originally published in 1970, is recognised to be part of Roland Barthes' 'post-structuralist' phase in which his concern for explicating systems of signs is overtaken by a desire to disrupt and decentre their authority. As a text, it signals the shift away from the use of the elements of formal semiology – or the guiding principles of structural linguistics – to study the real-world phenomena of cultural practices as images and texts that can be read. *Empire of Signs* could therefore be considered as a watershed in contemporary critical theory, given Barthes' position as a leading figure of French structuralism. Because of this theoretical and stylistic innovation, it is a key text of the period that ushers in and welcomes the 'post-structural' era of literary criticism.

Barthes developed his semiological method of reading the sign systems of culture after the work of linguists Ferdinand de Saussure, Louis Hjelmslev, Roman Jakobson and Emile Benveniste. The scope and depth of his work earned him a prestigious Chair in Literary Semiotics at the Collège de France. Like Claude Lévi-Strauss and Jean Piaget, Barthes influenced and was part of a generation of French critics and theorists interested in semiotics during the 1950s and 60s: Julia Kristeva, Michel Foucault, Jacques Lacan, Tzvetan Todorov, Jacques Derrida, Louis Althusser, Gilles Deleuze, Jean-François Lyotard, René Girard and Jean Baudrillard. This period of 'high structuralism' was marked by the fervour of great intellectual labour and intense public exchanges between the major figures of the movement that incubated various theoretical off-shoots such as deconstruction, narratology, archetypal criticism and structural Marxism. The critical importance of semiology lies in the fact that it enables theorists to create a *meta-*

language – a critical language or discourse – that is useful for analysing forms and structures of representation as parts encoded within the logic of a system. It posits multiple levels of signification (e.g., a letter, a word, a sentence, a punctuation mark) working singularly and together in relation to a coded, whole text. For this reason, semiology is also called a *formalist method* of analysis, since it links the expression of meaning or content within analysis to the elements of formal composition. Its theoretical precepts allow for the possibility of reading real and hypothetical levels of signification both 'above' and 'below' the sign, and of working out the relationships between them within a text.[2] The quest is to find and make accessible reserves of meaning within configurations of textual form. Consequently, signs, structures and codes are the main concerns of semiology in relation to the system of representation and its encoding of the elements of textuality.

What has been called Barthes' 'structuralist' phase encompasses texts such as *Writing Degree*

Zero, *Elements of Semiology* and *Mythologies*. The last of these books provides a theoretical exposition of his method of reading systems of signs in culture and their textual productions in the media. Some of the subjects that are taken up by Barthes during this period are advertisements, travel guides, fashion, photography, striptease and wrestling. The point is critically to interrogate the field of cultural products and practices so as to conduct an 'ideological critique bearing on the language of so-called mass-culture' and to 'analyze semiologically the mechanics of this language'.[3] For example, in another study of the period,[4] Barthes engages an advertisement for pasta to demonstrate the ideological interdependence of a system of lexical and visual signs and codes within the same text. We might call this type of analysis of image and text – also undertaken in *Empire of Signs* – a *cross-medial* approach. The objects depicted visually in the advertisement (spaghetti, tomato sauce, grated Parmesan cheese, onions, peppers and a string bag) can be grouped under the one lexical term used as the brand label for the product, /Panzini/. Not that these products are exclusive to a particular ethnicity, but in culinary terms, according to the advertisement, the ingredients for the 'complete spaghetti dish' are represented in the photograph as uniquely 'Italian' and therefore of excellent quality. The echo of cultural authenticity is in the origin of the name itself and its inflection of ethnic identity. Since the advertisement was designed for the French consumer, and not the Italian consumer, for Barthes the ethnic connotation of the name is particularly effective as a marketing tool to create desire and demand for the product by establishing a thematically meaningful context for the intended audience. The quality of the product is linked to the ethnicity of the name, thus evoking mythical images of an authentic Italian spaghetti dish that can be made right in one's own – in this case, French – home. The advertisement seems to suggest that all one need do is buy the product and relish the experience of cooking just like the Italians. It is rife with stereotypes latent within the form of representation. The 'Italianicity' of the products depends chiefly on a *contiguous*, or adjoined, relation between the word /Panzini/ and the products depicted, in order to achieve the transference of connotation from the lexical to the visual text, thereby resulting in *anchorage* and *relay*. The concepts of 'anchorage' and 'relay' that Barthes develops to analyse the interplay of word and image in the advertisement are useful for considering the way in which this 'combined code' type of text may generate and guide meaning-making semiotically. In anchorage, as Barthes explains, 'the text directs the reader through the signifieds of the image, causing him to avoid some and receive others ... It remote-controls him [or her] toward meaning chosen in advance'; whereas in relay, 'the text and image stand in a complementary relationship; the words in the same way as the images, are fragments of a more general syntagm and the unity of the message is realized at a higher level'.[5] In order to facilitate meaning, the message of the advertisement as a whole involves both the lexical–visual dependency of anchorage and the complementarity of both textual constituents found in relay.

Understanding Myth

Similarly to Barthes' analysis of the Panzini advertisement, his *Mythologies* highlights the critical task of the semiologist to demythify what is said and also unspoken in the representations of popular culture. That is, to debunk the bias of myths that are created or reinforced when the subject of culture itself takes the textual form of sign systems and codes. Ideology is at the core of mythology. Barthes' analysis of media in *Mythologies* reinforces the Marxist tenor of this theme.

Indeed, 'Myth Today', the last essay of the English version of *Mythologies*, which is an extended meditation on semiological method, uses the beliefs, desires and values expressed in the grand narratives of petit-bourgeois culture as a vehicle for demonstrating how to unlock the signifying structure of myth. Barthes shows that myth naturalises the idiosyncrasies of culture, universalises them, and makes them social norms through its rhetorical flourishes. *Mythologies* as 'ideology critique' exposes the ethical dilemma of leaving myth unexamined as a cultural substratum of what is natural and what is real in the life-world. The danger that Barthes sees in myth is that it allows layers of meaning to accumulate within its representations of culture, and encourages unreflective practices. Through myth, 'ideological abuse'[6] takes place because there is unquestioning faith in the message. The status quo of cultural norms is fed by the imagination of mythology. As Barthes says, the truth of myth characterises 'what-goes-without-saying'.[7] The cultural logic that is expounded through mythology attempts to reduce differences of interpretation and limit the excesses of meaning. Its ideological dimensions structure the terms of our responses to signs, texts and media representations and, more importantly, to history. Myths generalise experience to bring about a consensus on how we perceive reality, encounter the human condition, and act in respect to the difference of others as a community. The ethical, social and political boundaries of society and culture are framed by mythology. Myths provide interpretative archetypes for deciphering the meaning of the life-world we inhabit with a view to the present through the past. Mythology animates reality, translates and naturalises it for us, by infusing it with levels of ideological significance.

Wrestling with Myth

According to Barthes, myths give us critical models of understanding that we can use to map the meaning of experience by staggering one system atop another, to create two levels of interpretation. Both levels work singularly and in tandem, first to *highlight* reality and then to *gloss* reality. In *Mythologies*, Barthes shows how the primary level contains the 'factual' system of representation in which objects are signified. Barthes calls this the 'signifying plane'. It gives an alibi for keeping the form of representation separate from the content of representation. The secondary level promotes a symbolic system in which connections to meaning are made. Barthes calls this symbolic realm of associations *'le signifiant vide'* or 'empty signified'. It generates another plane of meaning beyond the cultural object or practice by giving representation the power of truth as presence. Empirical facts – buoyed with this *signifiant* presence – thus take on a metaphorical or symbolic lustre that seduces and thus causes the reader to jump from simply repeating mundane interpretations to making value judgements that have ethical and moral implications. That is why, Barthes explains, even though we know that the world of wrestling is a 'stage-managed sport',[8] its excessive spectacles of human experience – e.g., its exhibitions of pain, suffering, betrayal, guilt, treachery, cruelty, desire and elation – allow the viewer a purer identification with the actors. Emotion takes over, raw but not without an ideological bent. The audience quickly has to take sides for the spectacle of wrestling to be effective. As in mythology, in wrestling matches imaginary sagas of life-and-death struggles, pitting good against evil, are played out before an audience ready to identify within such a play the primordial ethical situations of the human condition. Wrestling exploits the mythological archetypes that preoccupy consciousness. A darkly masked figure, a face of evil, squares off against a crowd favourite who displays and defends all that is good in a culture. The mythical spectacle of wrestling relies on viewers' unconscious desire to work out the psychic and ethical tensions within the ideology of culture. It feeds on it. This symbolic element of identification – or gloss – demands the viewer's attention and accounts for the tremendous popularity of wrestling. For Barthes, myth distorts reality for ideological effect. It turns bias and prejudice into history. It quietly suspends the need for a questioning of representations in culture. Myth naturalises this distortion of reality and glosses over its rough-hewn text to make prevalent a point of view that can be taken on as a ready-made truth regarding existence.

Needless to say, Barthes does not trust myth. He believes its imaginary rendering of history, society and culture to be a cause of human self-deception when it becomes the source for truth. The contention is that mythology asserts itself as History when meaning needs to be fixed publicly, and reality demystified, for the sake of asserting claims to clarity and universal truth. Myth functions to resist the fragmentation of cultural memory by allowing us to take for granted all that is happening around us in everyday life. Reality is demystified for easy consumption. Myth exudes ideology because, Barthes concludes, it 'transform[s] meaning into form'.[9]

Post-structural Barthes

Whereas the early work of Barthes aims to unlock the secrets of representational forms such as mythology, the later work complicates the simplicity of that notion and even questions its relevance with respect to the cultural production of meaning. Signs, codes, structures and systems are still important in the later work, such as *Empire of Signs*, but as conventions to be played with and enjoyed. Gone are the inventories and labels that enabled Barthes, the semiologist, to produce a meta-language of inquiry. In *S/Z: The Pleasure of the Text and The Lover's Discourse*, for example, he is not so much interested in what is represented and how, as he is in generating new modes of reading for their own sake. Experiencing the *'jouissance'* of reading or the pleasurable release (sexual pun intended!) of engaging the difference of a text and playing with or enjoying it, becomes the critical objective. Meaning is secondary. It is halted by the emptiness of signs, their inability to stand outside of a conventional – and therefore arbitrary – system of representation that has produced them according to its own cultural logic. If anything, reading now becomes for Barthes a way to resist the power of a text over a reader, to question its motivation, and, ultimately, to engage its meaning. In other words, he wants to oppose the ideology of representational forms imposed upon a reader trapped within the semiological structures of a text. During this period, Barthes came to the conclusion that the best the critical reader could hope for were 'flashes' that illuminated an image or text but revealed nothing.

The linguistic elements of semiology as a reading strategy are displaced in Barthes' later work. Another set of critical preoccupations floods the vocabulary of his readings of cultural forms and practices. Barthes refocuses the critical lens of his theoretical arsenal on concepts related to the working-out of human desire. Thus, the emphasis of reading is placed on representations of the body, pleasure, love, possession, alienation, intersubjectivity, culture, difference, memory and writing. Interestingly enough, myth still occupies a central place in Barthes' post-structuralist phase as a form of meaning-making that allows him to read against the grain of cultural representations and the representation of culture.

The Empire of Empty Signs

As I stated earlier, *Empire of Signs* illustrates the shift in Barthes' later work. The text is more poetic than analytical, more reflective than critical. Barthes takes pleasure in playing with the narrative point of view by undercutting its validity so as to decentre its authority and disrupt its legitimacy. He wants to resist the temptation to mythologise his subject, Japan. That is, to idealise and naturalise an image of an Oriental culture as opposed to an Occidental one. The foreword that Barthes provides to *Empire of Signs* reads as follows:

The text does not 'gloss' the images, which do not 'illustrate' the text. For me, each has been no more than the onset of a kind of visual uncertainty, analogous perhaps to that loss of meaning Zen calls a satori. Text and image, interlacing, seek to ensure the circulation and exchange of these signifiers: body, face, writing; and in them to read the retreat of signs.[10]

In *Empire of Signs*, theory is embedded or grounded within the style of expression. There is no direct application of a method we could call 'semiological'. By consciously refusing to 'gloss' the images of Japan that he presents, Barthes avoids an appeal to the Western visual motif of light and darkness and its ideology. He forgoes its mythology and accepts the resulting loss of meaning, preferring not to attempt to enlighten the reader with the Truth about Japanese culture. Culture, if anything, is a retreat into signs for the sake of finding meaning within a system of signs whose reality is but a fiction of language – that is, an arbitrary way of coding and making sense of the world. Barthes, I think, would have agreed with this statement, given that his view of myth and its corresponding discourse, history, was indeed a sceptical one. History, like myth, produces cultural narratives that confuse the paths to making meaning of present events in relation to past occurrences. That is why Barthes refuses intentionally to gloss the text of *Empire of Signs* and its images: the effect would be to reproduce the ethnocentric myth of Japan that is its Western history.

There could be no other choice. What Barthes knows about Japan is always already filtered though 'an emptiness of language which constitutes writing'.[11] Meaning is delayed, access to truth prevented. On the one hand, the signs of Japan are empty for him, without natural referential meaning, so there can only be forms of representation that he does not fully understand. Mythology is thus avoided. The signs of Japan are just the signs of an empire. Or an empire of signs. On the other hand, as an outsider to Japanese culture, Barthes must locate himself within the ethnocentrism and cultural blindness of a narrow range of meanings that the image of Japan stimulates in the Western reader. Mythology is everywhere, but this time it comes from within him. It colours Barthes' responses to the signs he sees and experiences. 'Someday we must write the history of our own obscurity,' he says …

… *manifest the density of our narcissism, tally down through the centuries the several appeals to difference we may have occasionally heard, the ideological recuperations which have infallibly followed and which consist in always acclimating our incognizance of Asia by means of certain known languages (the Orient of Voltaire, the* Revue Asiatique, *of Pierre Loti, or of* Air France).[12]

Barthes' knowledge of Japan is limited to what he has read of its history and seen of its images, either through experience or in the media. This exposure to a Western archive of texts and images that are called 'Japan' establishes the *myth* of Japan as part of an Oriental culture as opposed to an Occidental culture. It is given a historical legacy that we call the 'History of Japan' which makes the cultural differences of

Japan comprehensible to the Western mind. This image of 'Japan' – its myth – is consequently an invention of the West. It bears no resemblance to the real Japan. It is a Western history of Japan. There is a reason to this representation of Japan that is produced outside of Japanese culture itself and that creates the Western mythology of 'Japan' – gives it its *exotic gloss*, Barthes would say – as part of an Oriental culture contrasted against a European culture. So, in one respect, nothing stands behind the empire of signs that Barthes calls Japan. Barthes' representation of Japan reflects the anxiety that the Western reader of culture feels when coming face-to-face with an unreadable text. The Japan of *Empire of Signs* should, in this sense, be called an *empire of empty signs*. The fact that the West 'moistens everything with meaning'[13] frustrates Barthes. It limits the ethics of reading to an excavation of the text for its significance. He therefore chooses to invent Japan, to write a fictional representation which does not have the pretensions of Truth and

History as its grounding. Missing are the transcendental signs of Western culture that depend on a metaphysical foundation of meaning: e.g., the Word, God, the Subject, the ego, presence, an immovable centre, and so on. Barthes can only relate the dizzying heterogeneity of Japan in a montage of images and texts that are striking in themselves. The experience of loss that he feels during his contact with the emptiness of its signs tempers his readings of cultural forms and practices. And yet, a question remains to be answered: Is it possible to write a history of Japanese culture without succumbing to reconstituting its Western mythology?

At first glance, it would seem not. But to attempt an answer to this question, we need to consider what problems the writing of cultural history poses for Barthes.

Culture and History

That all history can only be in the last analysis, the history of meaning, that is of Reason in general ... [14]

To invoke the other of the 'sign of history' is not to welcome an instant of madness that is without reason. Chaos or anarchy will always result from a critical stance away from an appeal to reason. If we choose to believe Jacques Derrida, even a history of madness would have its own idiosyncratic reasons, its own governing logic, whether we can fathom it or not. Nothing is without its own reason: no matter how misguided or unethical a thought or action might be. As Barthes has stated in 'The Discourse of History',[15] the loss of meaning is immanent to any history or representation of culture, because the signs of language intervene. Thus, writing about cultural events or practices can no longer be perceived to be an objective chronicling of details. History loses its facticity just by being written. History is a text. A glossy surface. A set of signs. History no longer documents 'the real', Barthes explains, but produces 'the intelligible'.[16] It is tempered by the cultural perspective of the historian in the process of interpreting and writing history.

The texts and images of history, like those of myth, are thoroughly penetrated by ideology and the rhetorical techniques of the historian. History is mediated by language and is therefore a mode of discourse that produces a text, but does not facilitate a representation of fact.

In *Specters of Marx: The State of the Debt, the Work of Mourning, and the New International*,[17] Derrida has taken a position similar to that of Barthes regarding the writing of history and ideology. Derrida criticises recent claims about the 'end of history' – made by liberal humanists such as Francis Fukuyama after the fall of Communism in Soviet Russia – as being nothing but an ideological confidence trick. That is, an attempt to rewrite history and influence cultural memory according to the political ideology of those who have a vested interest in eliminating differences of interpretation from a certain vision of civil society. For Derrida, reason is the ideology of history. History writes the emptiness of signs but glosses the images to fill in the gaps of understanding and thus make myth or ideology possible. Nothing more, nothing less.

Like myth, the central problem of writing the history of a culture is the problem of ideology. Barthes often returns to this theme in *Empire of Signs* – in fact, he never leaves it. His effort is to begin on a journey of learning about the difference of Japanese culture. The delay of this intellectual labour, he says, 'can only be the result of an ideological occultation'.[18] Barthes takes very seriously this responsibility to guide the reader through the images and texts of Japan as he sees it. One of the key ideas of *Empire of Signs* is how ideology is inextricably related to the question of meaning – the meaning of meaning. Barthes cannot escape his Western education and heritage. He cannot un-learn what he has already learned. This realisation brings semiotics into the picture, as the interpretation of meaning occurs in a field of articulation whose signs occupy what we can call the public sphere of culture. Barthes reminds us that 'Japan' as a signifier in the West involves the dissemination of signs and their mediation. The way in which these signs – images and texts – are represented is not haphazard. There is a historical legacy at work, motivated by ideology. This work comprises the translation of ideas, 'turns of mind', progression of thought, values and ideals of individuals, groups or societies embodied in various textualised forms across the diverse cultural milieus of different historical epochs that we call 'the West'. According to Barthes, there is a distinctive ideological purpose informing the operation of what he is doing by isolating 'certain features' forming a sign system called 'Japan': that is, writing a form of cultural history. It entails that the focus of interpretation be upon the textualised 'products' of culture and upon the contexts and practices within which their meanings, when inculcated socially, are distributed and 'consumed'.

Visualising Culture

That is why Barthes combines images within the text of *Empire of Signs*. The images contextualise the analysis, place it in history, give it a framework, as being based 'in reality'. The responsibility of representing the difference of Japan as a system of relations whose features Barthes identifies is consequently generated from the act of reading and writing the living spaces of these text–context relations. For example, mapping the Tokyo cityscape, exhibiting forms of writing, and depicting people in the act of bowing provide the reader with vignettes of Japanese cultural life. Visual representation concretises meaning articulated by and within the image that is portrayed. The ideology is laid bare, some would say. Its meaning is not hidden because the visual language of the picture anchors and relays the message. This point of view considers the image as an icon of content. It assumes one level of articulation, just like the trite saying, 'a picture is worth a thousand words'. This attitude is reminiscent of

Marshall McLuhan's famous dictum: 'The medium is the message.' In this case, we could replace 'medium' with 'picture' quite easily and come to conclusions echoed in the original neologism. The visual image does speak for itself, although not completely, since its total composition is made up of much smaller parts that articulate different levels of meaning depending on where one focuses one's gaze. All of the pictorial texts included in *Empire of Signs* supplement our general understanding of the narrative text, but there are multivalent levels of unexplored meaning.

What is more important for us, reading Barthes' rendering of the signs of Japanese culture, is the way in which the visual images – e.g., a Sumo wrestler, the geisha, a hand writing a Kanji character – establish a spatial and temporal record of the subjects depicted. The photograph becomes empirical proof of historical existence and at the same time an artefact of a moment past and forever lost.

Barthes examines the maddening effect of

this contradiction of meaning in *Camera Lucida*, his last book. He is intrigued by the way in which photographic realism collapses space and time, wherein significance is accumulated through the emptiness of the representation – what *is* and *is not* there in the here and now.

Empire of Signs forefronts the plenitude of meaning and the loss of meaning that is the problem of history, whether it is represented through words or visual images. In many ways, Barthes still has to intervene for the reader. Photographs and other visual images contextualise and complicate the difference between the Western myth of 'Japan' and the Japan that is a landscape of empty signs. What Derrida calls 'undecidability' is immanent to the space of interpretation. Culture influences the representation of history as well as the other way round. In other words, there is no recourse to a final, indisputable meaning. So, Barthes must highlight what he is explaining visually, to give it a pragmatic index, and show how it is rooted in the reality of cultural figures, spaces, and practices. But this does not provide a picture of truth. There is a world of difference between understanding examples and reproducing ideology, as Barthes reminds us by appealing to the discourse of history as a form of cultural mythology wherein truth can be found. Ultimately, however, the process of interpretation or meaning-making is left up to the reader. Ideology, like culture and subjectivity, is malleable. Its dimensions change with experience. Why can we say this?

Historical Method Before and After Ideology

Like Barthes, Louis Althusser identified ideology as an essential structure of cultural and historical life. It governs not only the means and modes of textualisation, but also the distribution, consumption and legitimation of meanings within social contexts. Ideology as a historical force constructs subjectivity. Of that there is no doubt. Yet it has limits. There is a fine line between the influence of ideology on consciousness and the possibility of totally reproducing its conceptual structures. Althusser has identified the nature of this 'relative autonomy' of ideology as it acts on subjectivity to determine the dominant ways in which we relate to external reality. He calls it 'interpellation', or the turn of attitudes, values and beliefs caused in an individual by the political apparatuses of State power. It is the defining moment when a 'citizen' becomes articulated as a 'subject'. But the limitations of this notion of ideology have been exposed in relation to human agency and history. For example, conscious and unconscious beliefs inform any form of action so as to render it directed, consequential, and therefore productive. The historian Hayden White explains:

Groups engage in political activities for political purposes, to be sure, but these activities are meaningful to them only by reference to some other, extrapolitical aim, purpose or value.

31

This is what permits them to imagine that their political activities are qualitatively different from those of their opponents or represent a higher value than those of their enemies. ... Historical events differ from natural events in that they are meaningful for their agents and variously meaningful to the different groups that carry them out.[19]

We cannot assume – and Barthes does not – that ideology works its way into the consciousness of each member of a culture in the same fashion. It is articulated within you and me through different means and ways. This accounts for the diversity of readings and interpretations between us. Ideology cannot occur without a web of resistance to its homogenising effects. Otherwise, we would all think and speak alike – and probably have nothing to talk or write about, since a total and tacit agreement would allow silence to prevail. As in telepathy, there would be nothing left to say that we would not already know. The need for communication would wither. All human action would be surmised in advance of its occurrence.

The importance of *Empire of Signs* is not so much in the detail of its analysis as in its expression of the Western anxiety that language means nothing, that meaning is not important. It is not surprising to Barthes – nor should it be to us – that the end of the nineteenth century could only have resulted in the extirpation of an ideologically-grounded interpretative framework from historical methodology. The entrenchment of a purely 'scientific' intention within the discipline was supported by a correspondence theory of truth. The signs of historical discourse were ultimately verifiable in their relation to reality. A logical language of propositions confirmed the truth of representation. An example of such a statement would be: 'Snow is white because snow is white.' There is no contradiction in the logic here, because it is based on empirical evidence which connects language to the external world causally. Three such perspectives for establishing the correspondence between the expression of concepts and their relation to reality have informed historiography since the nineteenth century. These are as follows. Language conceived as: 1) an index of causal relations governed by the materiality of external world structures (e.g., Marxist historical method); 2) an iconic, or *mimetic*, representation of external reality as reflected in the system of grammar and syntax, as well as the lexicon used to represent reality (e.g., the archetypal history of Ernst Cassirer); and 3) a motivated symbol of external reality which presupposes the presence of an overarching *Zeitgeist* (a 'Spirit of the Time') reflecting all aspects of a culture and thus revealing the essence of the whole (e.g., the Hegelian-influenced historians).

The privileging of a referential function within language displays the belief that the essence of the past is to be found in the wealth of detail that the historian documented, its undeniable 'facticity' and therefore its 'truthfulness'. The kernel of truth resides in the correspondence between the stories 'written' and the stories 'lived'. It is demonstrable only in the closely argued, causally-based logic of a dissertative style of address aimed at revealing the true story, a repeating of the actual events, and the 'real' story, the narrativised account of it. The use of a strictly narrative mode of historiography as a style of presentation is thus charged with endowing the representation of people, things and events with an illusory coherence. As Barthes shows, fundamentally, historical discourse becomes equivalent to the fictional discourse such as we might find in an epic, a novel or a play – where the drama of representation and the structuring of its exposition are more characteristic of an oneiric (dreamlike) reality than an actual one. That is why he has no qualms about writing of a fictional Japan – he must give a logic and coherence to his experience of it out of disjointed responses to the signs of its culture.

In 'The Discourse of History', Barthes has drawn attention to the principles of exposition governing the discipline of history and the circumstance of its utterance as a discourse. The distinction between 'fact' and 'fiction' in historiography lies with long-standing 'rules of evidence'. The validity of historical sources relies on links that can be readily traced to referents found in primary sources – e.g., textual archives (official documents, records of events, diaries, etc.) and 'relics' (material artefacts). Attempts at interpretation constitute the 'presentism' of non-objectively inclined historiographers, and are to be avoided at all costs. The materiality of these primary sources is conceived to confirm and anchor the authenticity of the contexts motivating their production, thereby attesting to the 'truth' of the historical reality referenced for the purpose of explaining the past or reconstructing it. Secondary sources – 'documentary' or second-hand accounts – if used at all, are to be carefully subjected to internal criticism first, in order to check the 'accuracy' and 'worth' of the statements contained according to laws of 'reason', probability, competence or bias. And then they are subjected to external criticism so as to verify the genuineness of the authorship or the originating context of the testimony. It should be noted that these procedural 'checks' may also be applied to primary sources if necessary.

In the end, history must render the contour of form or shape to a body of evidence. This involves reading and writing. Or an engagement with the signs of culture, as Barthes would say, where 'a shock of meaning is lacerated, extenuated to the point of its irreplaceable void'.[20] *Empire of Signs* decentres response and exposes the emptiness of the signs of writing in their relation to what Japan as a culture really is. In this sense, for Barthes, his real-life subject is a 'novelistic object',[21] one that allows him to situate the focus of inquiry directly within the semiotic process of reading and writing Japanese culture. *Empire of Signs* problematises the precepts of a correspondence theory of history that posit the 'truth' of the past to be manifest in the relation between the representational surface of discourse and its conceptual content. A critical practice such as Barthes' cannot but deconstruct the genealogy of historical meaning like the earlier work of Michel Foucault, in which questions concerning cultural representation and ideology are taken up via an examination of the Western archaeologies of knowledge and its orders of discourse. *Empire of Signs* reminds us that the source of meaning-making potential in historiography is actualised within the semiological features of its production as the reading and writing of culture. Barthes forces us to accept Derrida's exhortation to look for 'nothing outside the text'. The representation of individuals and events in the discourse of history constitutes nothing but signs engaging a reader. No claims to facticity, objectivity or truth can be made outside of the margins of the text. The signs of history are empty. We must accept the logic that Barthes offers, given his admission that 'what is presented here does not appertain (or so it is hoped) to art, to Japanese urbanism, to Japanese cooking. The author has never, in any sense photographed Japan.'[22]

Scrutinising the writing of history requires the historiographer's active intellectual engagement with the world as text – as signs – not facts. Replacing the concepts 'word' and 'representation' with the concepts 'sign' and 'signification' places the question of the production, distribution and consumption of meaning decisively in a semiological realm of analysis. The tendency to discern text–context relations on the basis of distinguishing the 'real' from the 'imaginary' is suspended because there are no clear distinctions. Language will always mediate understanding. And fundamental questions arise about the nature and possibility of accessing meaning outside of discourse: What does 'reality' look like outside of discourse? How would we access it independently of language? How do we know when it has been accessed without its re-inscription in discourse? How do we know whether our views of it are faithful to it? And so on. In semiological terms, such questions seek to determine the nature of an extra-discursive reality. But can we ever escape the ideology that colours perspective? I think not. Historical discourse must then be, in some shape or form, a fictional mode of representation. In 'The Discourse of History', Barthes asked:

Does the narration of past events, which, in our culture from the time of the Greeks onwards, has generally been subject to the sanction of historical 'science', bound to the underlying standard of the 'real', and justified by the principles of 'rational' exposition – does this form of narration really differ, in some specific trait, in some indubitably distinctive feature, from the imaginary narration, as we find it in the epic, the novel, and the drama?[23]

He goes on to say that 'in "objective" history, the "real" is never more than an unformulated signified, sheltering behind the apparently all-powerful referent. This situation characterizes what might be called the *realistic effect (effet du réel)*.'[24] When analysing diverse modes of discourse production, there is a common semiological principle of reading that quickly becomes evident. Meaning is created in relation to the arbitrary differences between constituent signs removed from reality. Signs stand for something else other than themselves. Ideology is involved in their creation. Signs supplement reality and interpret it arbitrarily through the effect of pointing to differences of form that allow us to make meaning of those differences for the purposes of identifying and comprehending what signs refer to in the external world. Because ideology influences perception and therefore the reading and writing of history, instability characterises the signified–signifier relations posed within its textual representations of culture. Access to the real is deferred. The meaning of culture is decentred. Truth disperses and any trace of the possibility for the closure of interpretation is lost. If history is fiction, can we call it a lie? This would reflect quite badly on Barthes and the representation of Japan that he puts forward in *Empire of Signs*.

Lies, Fiction, Ideology

In *Empire of Signs*, Barthes brings to the critical forefront the problem of analysing history and therefore culture, or the cultural history of Japan, from a seemingly objective point of view. How does one write from the perspective of one who knows the Truth about Japanese cultural history? There can be no such unbiased and omniscient point of view. The hope of a radical semiotic confrontation with History and its uncritical representational apparatus is the possibility that the basis for the authority of Western culture and the truth of its discourse can be 'deconstructed'. So, can we still call *Empire of Signs* a cultural history? We need a little more background to answer this question.

Barthes engages neither in a 'deconstruction' nor a 'demystification' of Japan or its culture, if such a thing were possible. But, like Derrida, through the act of writing he elicits the theoretical preconditions for rethinking cultural history after the semiotic turn of the 1950s and 60s. This critical move beckons us to acknowledge history and its representation of culture as an interpretative act: an act of writing and thus of representation. Semiotics turns history into historiography – *the writing of history*. There is a difference. Barthes makes us aware of the way in which the authority of history in the West is bound to the logic of the metaphysical *logos*, as the ancient Greeks called it. The *logos* is *the mystical power of the Word of God* that enfleshes meaning and reason in the Word. History is the Word. The reason of History is the Reason of the Word. And this presupposition enables a vision of culture recorded as history and history recorded as culture – that is, a writing of cultural history through which the meaning of culture is codified in a system and represented as the Truth. Above all, we must remember that history has an 'intellectual' or 'cultural' history. It has its own systems of signification and codes of meaning-making, to which we must now turn before going any further in reading Barthes' writing of the *Empire of Signs*.

Since its inception by the German philosopher Hegel under the rubric of *Geistesgeschichte*, cultural history has traditionally identified a particular sub-genre of general historiography. It has been faithful to the 'master' discipline in its adherence to the same theoretical precepts, but has differed in the transdisciplinary breadth of its sources. For example, philosophy, anthropology, sociology, linguistics, psychology and even literary theory have contributed to the analytical methodology of cultural history. This mixing of methods has definitely contributed to the confusion about what the discipline of cultural history actually entails. The problem of the autonomy of cultural history in the field of historically oriented studies of culture is compounded by the fact that it lacks a 'proper name'. It is called intellectual history or the history of ideas, also cultural history, in the United States. The French term for it is *l'histoire des mentalités*. In Russia, it is referred to as the history of thought. There is great significance to the fact that cultural history lacks a proper name. This heterogeneity fails to mark clearly the boundaries for its own identity within a well-defined disciplinary space. Therefore it does not establish its unique sense of selfhood in such a way as to legitimise both the difference of its scope and of its method. In other words, there is no clear consolidation of origins or ends within cultural history. This dilemma has caused a crisis of representation within the larger discipline of history, and more specifically, regarding the truth of the historical text.

The need to legitimise the diversity of methods within cultural history, as a sub-genre of history, reveals a latent anxiety of influence concerning the autonomy of its disciplinary identity. There is a nagging perception of a splintered *corps*. Barthes reiterates this when he says that the perspective of history merges with the concerns of the humanities in its turn to culture as a subject. The sense of disciplinary dislocation among those who write cultural history, and write *about* it, has necessitated a rethinking of its guiding principles. *Empire of Signs* is an example of Barthes' working-out of the practice of writing history and representing culture – or writing cultural history with a post-structural twist. His aim is not to secure a disciplinary identity for cultural historiography, nor is the text a model for historical writing. It merely indulges Barthes' 'fantasy' as a writer. It tests his power to create an empire of signs: a text; his own aesthetic vision of 'Japan'; a semio-logical utopia where representation is not 'over-fed' by the Western imperative for meaning. Japan as an empire of *empty* signs speaks to his own experience of the culture. That is why Barthes is fascinated with Japan. It is a chance to upset the careful metaphysics of the West, an opportunity to immerse himself as a theorist and a writer in an empire of signs where all around him he sees the innocence of representation. Above all, it is a chance for Barthes to learn something he does not already know. For example, in Japanese culture, 'sexuality is in sex, not elsewhere; in the United States, it is the contrary; sex is everywhere, except in sexuality', he observes.[25] Elsewhere, Barthes states that, contrary to what the tourist guide books say, Japanese flower arrangement is not concerned with the 'rigorous constructions' of symbolism, but simply with the aesthetic production of liveable space – the beauty of natural colour and form admired for its own sake. Referring to the logic of giving a gift, Barthes observes that in Japanese culture the point is not what it contains: 'the triviality of the thing' is 'put off' by being 'wrapped with as much sumptuousness as a jewel'.[26] Western cultural *topoi* are upset in these examples.

Barthes describes *Empire of Signs* as containing 'happy mythologies'. No ethical intervention into the cultural logic of representational forms and practices is required. Barthes could not do that from his vantage point, given that he is an outsider looking at, and into, signs that both signify and negate the possibility of an empirical 'Japan'. The situation facilitates writing without a pretext. The text facilitates the expression of Barthes' semiological adventure with the signs of Japan, an empire of signs – Japan as an empire of signs. More than once, Barthes comments on the emptiness of the signs around him. He cannot penetrate the reality that they represent. He just reacts to the signs. The journey of writing is a 'descen[t] into the untranslatable, to experience its shock without ever muffling it, until everything Occidental in us totters and the rights of the "father tongue" vacillate'.[27] *Empire of Signs* reflects Barthes' attempt to transgress the cultural boundaries of historical writing and semiology. As a student immersed in the empire of signs, he wants to escape 'that tongue which comes to us from our fathers and proprietors of a culture which, precisely, history transforms into "nature"'[28] – and which forges myth when we want to appeal to a generalisable human experience. Barthes claims as a right the power of invention in representing Japanese culture, if for no other reason than to work out his own understanding of the culture and its signs. He wants to resist the temptation to idealise and mythify Japan. To Barthes, Japan is an empire of signs that 'allows [him] to "entertain" the idea of an unheard-of symbolic system, one altogether detached from our own'.[29] Specifically nationalistic conceptualisations of culture and history are rejected by him. Barthes wants to incite 'the possibility of difference, of mutation, of a revolution in the propriety of symbolic systems'.[30] Such a critical move would suspend the need to locate Japan in opposition to Western culture and therefore naturalise it as part of a mythological 'Orient'. Barthes is looking to put forward a representation of difference that yields a plurality of definitions and conceptual tools, and that avoids creating cultural stereotypes. *Empire of Signs* pushes back the traditional disciplinary boundaries of cultural history by showing its limitations.

However, Barthes is not totally successful in avoiding naïve or idealised representations of Japanese culture. And that is the risk he must take, knowing that its implications are immeasurable to the ethics of reading. What would be worse for Barthes would be to reinforce the mythology of Japan that is premised on the biased representations of the Orient prevalent in Western cultural ideology. The following are illustrations of the lapses that Barthes succumbs to. Cooked rice 'is the only element of weight in all of Japanese alimentation … it is what sinks in opposition to what floats'.[31] During preparation, 'its substantial destination is the fragment, the clump, the volatile conglomerate'.[32] Even more puzzling is the remark that '[t]he Japanese face is without moral hierarchy'.[33] Barthes makes this declaration after a long anatomical meditation on what he calls 'the Japanese eye' as compared to 'the Western eye'. This conceptual opposition repeats what Derrida has called the binary logic of Western metaphysics, in which two items are set in opposition so as to enable their conceptualisation, and thus to gauge their value, through the identification of differences between them. Barthes' characterisation of the Japanese face as lacking a 'moral hierarchy' is no doubt precipitated by an ethical reaction to a comparison between physiologies. The conclusion is so steeped in Western representations of the Orient that it borders on naïve racism. Ironically, it is only in the opposition of the Japanese face and its otherness to 'Occidental ideology' that Barthes finds value.

And yet, despite its inability to defy totally the Western representation of Japan, Barthes' text is well beyond what we might call the standard practices of reading culture and writing its history. This is because Barthes acknowledges the limitations of his own perspective. *Empire of Signs* thereby leaves open the possibility for a reassessment of historical methodology in relation to questions of culture and its representation after semiotics. Can we ask for more?

Signing Off

As we have seen, in the foreword to *Empire of Signs* Barthes alludes to the breaking of new disciplinary ground regarding what constitutes the truth of the texts and images comprising the writing of history and culture. History is redefined as a culturally arbitrary narrative; or an ideologically determined discourse of experience conceived within a narrow interpretative frame of reading and writing, and all that that entails in terms of the subjective act of making of meaning from texts and images. 'Japan' – as a historical place-marker in *Empire of Signs* – is an empty sign. Its essence is elusive. The narrative that Barthes produces is therefore more 'fictitious' than an accurate depiction of Japanese cultural history. The images presented are not designed to make life stand still for easy observation of the difference between the Occident and the Orient.

Barthes is very conscious of the fact that his cultural history of Japan is a 'situation of writing'.[34] *Empire of Signs* is a record of personal experience, a journal of the short trip that Barthes took to a country called Japan. Its significance is in the process of writing as a moment of reflection on the substance of experience, rather than in the truth of the message. Barthes writes his cultural history of Japan from a Western point of view which he cannot simply put aside or step back from. He is always already inside this situation of writing from the location of one to whom the experience of being a foreigner is ever present here. Its effects already filter his perception of the country he visited, its people and traditions. *Empire of Signs* is a way for Barthes to come to grips with the *otherness of Japan* and the exotic ideal of its cultural history as seen from a Western viewpoint. Reflection must begin from the relative isolation of this position which he exemplifies as a visitor to Japan. The anxiety of this situation of writing that Barthes identifies is the sense of being *far away, lost* in the emptiness of the signs whose essence he cannot hope to understand but must idealise to make history the point of cultural difference. History in *Empire of Signs* is therefore historiography, or the writing of history. Barthes does not represent empirical truth – if for no other reason, because he cannot hope to do it in *Empire of Signs*. According to Barthes, its discourse appeals to empirical truth, but its monuments – texts and images – are the products of an emptiness within language. Japan exemplifies the lack of this signifying potential that Barthes attempts to understand, or complicate his notion of. There is an essential difference between the discipline of history and its practice of historicising reality, a difference that is accentuated and magnified by the semiological perspective that Barthes uses to read and write the texts of Japanese culture in *Empire of Signs*. Because history cannot write itself to record the archive of itself without the necessity of human intervention, there is a loss of absolute meaning at the origin of writing, whereby the truth of history is supplanted by the veil of language. Viewing history as the *writing of history* is tantamount to ushering in the 'semiotic turn' of history, thus opening up history to the problems of reading its texts and the influences on its texts.

In the foreword to *Empire of Signs*, Barthes alludes to the inevitability of this epistemological rupture or break that his text causes with the discipline of history, and the gradual erosion of the discourses of authority that authenticate and mythify the grounds of its truth value. History is a text written to be read by others. It mediates for our understanding of real or perceived events and their effects by providing an organising point of view to an empirical body of source information. As a text that reads and represents the occurrences of the life-world, history is the subjective nature and cultural arbitrariness of the forms of its representations that gloss its truth because of the impossibility of objective representation or direct access to reality. The ground of history is a field of contested texts and images to be read and written about *like a fiction or a dream in which there is an experiencing of the uncanny or a feeling of estrangement when one is in contact with an other*. Barthes reads and writes the difference of Japanese history and its culture in *Empire of Signs*. But he cautions us against reading his text as a Master Text that allows Western readers to experience the essential differences of Japanese culture. *Empire of Signs* is rather a subjective rendering of his travels in, and exposure to, the texts and images of Japan. No representation – either in visual images or in words – can retrieve the essence of a culture and the meaning of its history, because the loss of meaning is always already there at the origin of the experience. *Empire of Signs* can be nothing but a product of Barthes' imagination dealing with the excesses of meaning produced by the trauma of cultural dislocation and estrangement. Japan is 'a fictive nation'[35] in this sense, an empire of signs from which Barthes produces meaning. Access to truth is always already lost to the semiological and ideological forces influencing and filtering our

perceptions of the world and therefore con-
structing the dimensions of our realities. Barthes
'in no way claim[s] to represent or analyze
reality itself (these being the major gestures of
Western discourse)'.[36] Instead, he will isolate 'a
certain number of features'[37] from which a system will be formed. As Barthes explains, '[i]t is
this system which I shall call: Japan'.[38] That is
why Barthes is resigned to producing a textual
'circulation and exchange' of signifiers con-
nected to the body, the face, and writing. Each
of these entities marks the concatenation of a
visible language to be read by an other. All are
texts – tissues of experience produced by and
producing layers of signifying possibilities. The
body, the face and writing are the domains of
an other and metaphors for the presence and
absence of meaning or its progressive loss
within a symbolic system of difference. In the
foreword, Barthes fixates upon a mode of
reading suitable to his text and its interlacing
of words and images. It tells us how to predis-
pose ourselves to its writing. How, then, do we

read Barthes and the *Empire of Signs*? The answer lies in reading the retreat of the signs of history as the writing of culture for flashes of insight into the complexity of representing the experience of reality, the reality of experience. Nothing more, nothing less.

Notes

1. Roland Barthes, *Empire of Signs*, trans. Richard Howard, New York: Hill and Wang, 1982, p. 108.

2. Barthes explains the semiotic imperative towards identifying various levels of analysis in *Elements of Semiology*, trans. Annette Lavers and Colin Smith, New York: Hill and Wang, 1981.

3. Roland Barthes, *Mythologies*, select. and trans. Annette Lavers, London: Paladin, 1973, p. 9.

4. Roland Barthes, *Image–Music–Text*, ed. and trans. Stephen Heath, New York: Hill and Wang, 1977.

5. Ibid., pp. 40–1.

6. Barthes, *Mythologies*, p. 11.

7. Ibid., p. 11.

8. Ibid., p. 15.

9. Ibid., p. 142.

10. Barthes, *Empire of Signs*, p. xi.

11. Ibid., p. 4.

12. Ibid., p. 4.

13. Ibid., p. 70.

14. Jacques Derrida, 'Cogito and the History of Madness', in *Writing and Difference*, trans. Alan Bass, Chicago: University of Chicago Press, 1978, p. 308.

15. Roland Barthes, 'The Discourse of History', in E.S. Schaffer (ed.), *Comparative Criticism: Vol. 3. A*

Year Book, trans. S. Bann, Cambridge: Cambridge University Press, 1981, pp. 3–20.

16. Ibid., p. 18.

17. Jacques Derrida, *Specters of Marx: The State of the Debt, the Work of Mourning, and the New International*, trans. Peggy Kamuf, New York and London: Routledge, 1994.

18. Barthes, *Empire of Signs*, p. 4.

19. Hayden White, *The Content of the Form: Narrative Discourse and Historical Representation*, Baltimore: Johns Hopkins University Press, 1987, p. 210.

20. Barthes, *Empire of Signs*, p. 4.

21. Ibid., p. 3.

22. Ibid., p. 4.

23. Barthes, 'The Discourse of History', p. 7.

24. Ibid., p. 17.

25. Ibid., p. 29.

26. Ibid., p. 46.

27. Ibid., p. 6.

28. Ibid., p. 6.

29. Ibid., p. 3.

30. Ibid., pp. 3–4.

31. Ibid., p. 12.

32. Ibid., p. 12.

33. Ibid., p. 102.

34. Ibid., p. 4.
35. Ibid., p. 3.
36. Ibid., p. 3.
37. Ibid., p. 3.
38. Ibid., p. 3.

Select Bibliography

Roland Barthes, *Writing Degree Zero*, trans. Annette Lavers and Colin Smith, New York: Hill and Wang, 1967.

Roland Barthes, *Elements of Semiology*, trans. Annette Lavers and Colin Smith, New York: Hill and Wang, 1981.

Roland Barthes, *Mythologies*, select. and trans. Annette Lavers, London: Paladin, 1973.

Roland Barthes, *Camera Lucida: Reflections on Photography*, trans. Richard Howard, New York: Hill and Wang, 1977.

Roland Barthes, *Image–Music–Text*, ed. and trans. Stephen Heath, New York: Hill and Wang, 1977.

Roland Barthes, *The Fashion System*, trans. Matthew Ward and Richard Howard, New York: Hill and Wang, 1983.

Roland Barthes, *Michelet*, New York: Hill and Wang, 1987.

Roland Barthes, 'The Photographic Message', in *Barthes: Selected Writings*, trans. Stephen Heath, Glasgow: Fontana, 1989, pp. 194–210.

Websites

The Voice of the Shuttle: Web Page for Humanities
Research: http://vos.ucsb.edu/

Cultural Studies Center: www.popcultures.com

Key Ideas

Culture

Culture is a highly ambiguous notion. It has contra-
dictory connotations depending on its use and the
context in which it appears. For some, it conveys
different notions of aesthetic, intellectual or artistic
accomplishment, e.g., Matthew Arnold's descrip-
tion of poetry as 'the best that has been thought and
said'. In its more anthropological dimensions, culture functions not as an arbitrary 'standard of
excellence' but as a generalised way of living which
displays and exhibits the application of certain
value and belief systems reflected within human
actions and institutions. In the context of Cultural
Studies, the latter notion is the more prevalent. If
we conceive of the natural world and its phenomena
as a realm without human intervention, then
'culture' means all things produced by human intervention: structures of government, communication
technologies, language, political ideologies, reli-
gion, educational institutions, social customs and
so on. Jean-Jacques Rousseau has argued that even
'nature' as an image of existence with or without
culture is a conception that could only have been
produced by culture. Yet it is also conceivable to

argue that humanity and all its trappings exist within nature, however different surface impressions seem. At times, there is an assumption that 'culture' refers to human productions that are not mediated by economic or ideological interests, but this representation of culture quickly breaks down when cultural productions are seen to serve means and ends other than the sole act of creation itself. For example, a painting acquires a certain monetary value because it was painted by a specific individual. Rather than being given away, it is auctioned off or sold. The act of painting as an act of cultural production is permeated by the conditions of economic exchange that determine the value of the cultural object.

Ideology

Originally coined by the philosopher Destutt de Tracy in the early nineteenth century, 'ideology' was used to describe a 'science of ideas' that could reveal unconscious tendencies of the psyche that influence human behaviour, like prejudice and class consciousness. Later on, Karl Marx and Karl Mannheim introduced the word into the discourse of modern sociology. It has now come to signify a range of conceptions related to the social production of consciousness, though usually without the subjective awareness of its operation. Fredric Jameson has called it the foundation of the political unconscious, while for Louis Althusser it is what creates subjectivity through the interpellation of consciousness by the State Ideological Apparatus. It signals any of the following preoccupations of mind: values, beliefs, expectations, ideals, a world view and horizons of understanding. Ideology is an interpretative device – a filter of perception – used by subjectivity to make sense of the world around it. Ideology can be shared when it becomes articulated as social action via human agency. For Marxist thought, ideology is a distortion of reality because it creates a 'false consciousness'. In *Literary Theory: An Introduction*, Terry Eagleton defines ideology as 'those modes of feeling, valuing, perceiving and believing which have some kind of relation to the maintenance and reproduction of social power'. Ideology functions to naturalise everything that is economic, political and social, and historically so as to make its contingency appear apolitical and timeless. The process of ideological interpellation is unconscious, and creates myths like 'common sense'. This appearance of the 'naturalness' of an idea is called the ideological effect.

Meta-history

Meta-history is, generally, the philosophy of history that considers the principles giving rise to the notion of historical progression and that refers to the narratives that describe this. More specifically, it is a book by Hayden White describing historical writing (or historiography) in terms analogous to those of meta-fiction and meta-narrative: that is, a writing of history which is self-conscious of its own rhetorical styles and forms of writing. White contends that an objective history is impossible. He likens the discourse of history to a narration of events not unlike that found in a fictional text. Meta-history as such raises questions about the power of representation, the influence of ideology on narration, and the act of writing.

Meta-language

Meta-language is essentially language about other language. In semiotic analysis, the language under investigation is called the 'object language', while the language created or used to perform the investigation is identified as the 'meta-language'. For post-structuralists, the very notion of a meta-language is anathema to the possibility of interpretative openness, possibly because it seems to be a means of universalising experience: the implication is that meta-languages can be used to explain how a model reader/viewer responds to a model text. There is no accounting for differences of interpretation. Semiotics calls these aberrant readings – in other words, readings that are not in keeping with the codic thrust of the text and its structures. Umberto Eco maintains that a text produces its own model reader. The point of reading is therefore somewhat determined by the structures and codes that a reader engages. To achieve a state of objectivity, a meta-language would have to stand outside history and therefore be immune to ideological effects. The notion of a meta-language contradicts the premises of semiotics if we consider Eco's observation. How could language divest itself of its contextual motivation?

Myth

In addition to the usual connotations of fable, folk-lore, legends, superstitions, etc., 'myth' has taken on several implications in contemporary theory. As we have seen while engaging with the work of Roland Barthes, myth is the result of ideology. Cultural products and practices are dehistoricised so as to universalise their significance and make them seem natural to human experience. The meanings of what mythologies imply are, however, not natural. They serve the particular interests of a controlling culture which uses myth to promote cultural reproduction. There are innumerable examples, but arguably the most basic one in the field of literary studies in English is the canon of master texts that define the characteristics of what good literature is. The plays of Shakespeare have taken on this function in English studies, to the point where Harold Bloom has stated that 'the Bard' has taught 'us' all we need to know about Western culture. In fact, he invented it and showed us in the West how to read and represent it.

Representation

At a basic level, a representation is merely a thing which is represented through the assistance of something else – e.g., the colour black represents death, while the colour green represents life. Representation is a vehicle by which two unrelated things are brought together to signify a concept. This view of representation has it as a sort of correspondence in essence to the thing represented. Most contemporary forms of critical thought would reject this assumption, albeit on different grounds.

Critiques have therefore arisen to challenge the conventional assumptions of communication as a naïve form of representation. For example, Jacques Derrida has complicated the idea of representation by coining the term *différance* to explain how interpretation takes place by both the difference and deferral of meaning. *Différance* enables us to rethink representation as not just the placing together of two different things – a concept with signifier – but as the deferral of meaning that happens when signs intervene, be it through speaking or writing. For Derrida, representation cannot be *re*-presentation because there can be no motivational, contiguous, analogical or relational connection between what a sign is and what it represents. Even though meaning is made by distinguishing the differences among signs, it is always deferred from its original sources.

Sign
Ferdinand de Saussure identified the sign to be an element of language composed of the relationship between a signifier (a sound-image, e.g., a phoneme or morpheme) and a signified (a concept expressed or an object referred to). Although the Saussurean model was more influential in the development of

French structuralism, the American philosopher Charles Sanders Peirce had a fully developed conceptualisation of the sign. For Peirce, a sign is an element of language or an image composed of the relationship between the sign itself, a referent (the object to which the sign refers), the ground of representation (the nature of the relationship to the referent), and the interpretant (the experiential relationship between the interpreter and the meaning). The sign refers to a referent within a field of representations that ground the sign according to its function – what it refers to and how, for what purpose. Meaning is made when the reader of the sign decodes the ground of representation so as to interpret the difference between signs from experience. Despite the differences between Saussurean and Peircean semiotics, as alluded to above, a sign can have no motivational, contiguous, analogical or relational connection to what it represents. A sign is always arbitrary, otherwise it would represent itself, which in turn determines whether the sign is what Peirce called an icon, an index, or a symbol.